MW00326196

POWERFUL . . . MOVING, INSPIRATIONAL! These stories of real-life situations will bring **hope, encouragement, and restoration** to those who have found themselves in circumstances beyond their control. An important book for hurting souls.

--Bill Glass, President/Founder
Bill Glass Ministries

As a National Missionary of 24 years with Christian Women's Clubs, I have read and heard thousands of touching, life-changing testimonies. The **unforgettable testimonies** in this book are not only dynamic and heartwarming but give the reader ways to solve life's complexities with God's grace. The Lord Jesus Christ and his Word, the Bible, are glorified. It's **a must reading** for everyone--a book you won't be able to put down.

--Mary Adams, National Representative
Stonecroft Ministries

As Lori's pastor, I watched her and Brent walk though some very dark days and come through in victory. As you read this marvelous account of God's protection and grace, you, too, **will be encouraged** to allow the Lord to direct your steps.

--Ted Kersh, Pastor
Oklahoma City, OK

These testimonies are powerful examples of God's ability to change lives and to provide all that we need. This is **a faith-building book** for everyone.   --Charlie Duke
Apollo 16 Astronaut

Ordinary Women...
Extraordinary
Circumstances

Bonnie Lang
Margolyn Woods
Pat Breckenridge
Lori Trice

(Compiled by Margolyn Woods)

Copyright © 1996 by

Milton Publishing Company, Inc.
P.O. Box 6
Lookout Mountain, Tennessee 37350
706-820-1060

Printed in the United States of America

ISBN 1-879908-09-3

Editor Carol G. Martin, Chattanooga, TN

The four women whose testimonies appear in this book are active on the Christian Speakers Circuit at conferences, retreats, workshops, luncheons, and dinners. Along with sharing their testimonies, they speak on numerous other topics. If you would like to contact them regarding speaking engagements, please write in care of **Milton Publishing Company**, P.O. Box 6, Lookout Mountain, TN 37350.

Bonnie Lang	Dealing With Disappointment
	When God Says, "NO!"
	Praying For Your Children
	The Virtuous Woman
	Marriage As A Ministry
Margolyn Woods	Beauty From Within
	Marriage 101
Pat Breckenridge	Grace In Grief
	Sitting At The Feet Of Jesus
	Using Our Gifts For His Glory
	Joy In The Crisis
	The Ministry of Encouragement
	Lifting Up The Cross
	Expectations
Lori Trice	God Is Sufficient
	Living As A Godly Woman
	A Different Kind of Marriage

Dedication

This book is dedicated to all of the people in our lives who took the time to share the gospel of Jesus Christ.

Psalms 96:3   Tell of His glory among the nations, His wondrous deeds among all the people.

Special Thanks

A special thanks to Bill and Vonnete Bright for inspiring this book. It was ten years ago that my husband Roy and I met this lovely couple. One of the first things Dr. Bright said to me was, "Margolyn, tell me how you came to know Jesus Christ as your personal Savior." This started my life-long quest of hearing and sharing personal testimonies of God's love.

Contents

Foreword

Almost 50 years of my life has been dedicated to helping fulfill the Great Commission of our Lord Jesus Christ--winning and discipling others according to **2 Timothy 2:2**. In this worldwide ministry, I have discovered that the most powerful way to communicate the gospel is through personal testimony. Nonbelievers as well as believers are drawn to testimonies of what life was like before meeting Christ, how the individuals met the Lord Jesus, and of the miracles of His grace as they began their new lives in Him. **"If any man be in Christ, he is a new creature. All things are passed away and behold all things have become new."** -- 2 Corinthians 7:14.

In this book, Margolyn has compiled heartwarming, tear-jerking, will-moving testimonies of what God has done in the lives of four women. Jesus said **"Follow Me and I will make you to become fishers of men."** The book will motivate believers to be more faithful in following Jesus and bringing others to Him. I highly recommend it to everyone--men and women, believers and nonbelievers.

     Bill Bright, Founder and President
     Campus Crusade for Christ International

Bonnie Lang

There we were standing at the altar about to be married. Jim was my dream, my white knight, young, handsome, and ambitious. He was an upstanding graduate of the Air Force Academy, a pilot who was ready to take on the world and all it had to offer.

He was everything I had always wanted in a man, and I knew that he would love me, care for me, and meet all of my needs. He would provide for me financially; I'd never have to worry about making a living. He would take care of my need for self-worth; I would have his support in all that I tried to accomplish, and he would be the perfect mate in every way. Therefore, I would be totally fulfilled as a woman.

Of course his thoughts were similar. He had found the perfect wife. His young bride would take care of all his needs: no more laundry to worry about, no more meals to cook. She would satisfy his sex drive and would always look up to and adore him. What great expectations we had!

The first few years of our marriage were marked by the zeal to succeed. Jim was promoted early, highly

respected and sought after as an Air Force officer. I pursued
my career as a teacher. After only two years, I was awarded
"Outstanding Young Woman of the Year" in our state for
my accomplishments in the classroom and community. We
worked hard but eventually we felt unfulfilled in the Air
Force; consequently, Jim decided to change careers and
venture into the business world. Jim had always wanted to
have his own company and be his own boss, so we left the
Air Force and moved to California to pursue our dreams.

As we sat in our newly purchased home, with our
first baby girl, we listed our ambitions and dreams. Heading
the list was Jim's goal to make a million dollars before he
was 40. In addition, we wanted to travel, buy vacation
homes, sports cars, and airplanes. We wanted more
children, more money, status in the community, and . . .
more, more, more!

We spent the next few years in pursuit of these
dreams and saw them met one by one! By the time Jim was
32, he had accomplished all of his life's goals.

In the process, we discovered that what the world told us would make us happy and bring us pleasure had left us unfulfilled and malcontent. The planes, cars, cruises, lovely homes, titles, honors, prestige and money were only temporary pleasures. Our relationship had suffered terribly. Extremely long hours at the office had kept Jim away from his home and family. Our four young girls hardly knew or saw their father because he left before dawn and came home long past their bedtimes at night.

We lived in quiet desperation as Jim's ambitions pushed him further and further away from his family and toward the elusive dream we sought. His "Type A" personality and drive for stature in the business community, coupled with my resentment and unsupportive attitude, was driving a wedge deep into our relationship. Seemingly, there was nothing to hold the two of us together as we led our separate lives.

While Jim was out pursuing the "American dream," the demands of four children under six years of age occupied my time and energy. I spent lonely nights at home, frustrated and disillusioned. Our moments together were punctuated by "discussions" about when we would get out of the "rat race" and have time together. Many were the days when our children and I would be packed and waiting to depart for our vacation home that Daddy would call and tell us to go on without him. Vacations in our lovely mountain home were often empty and sad. I found myself becoming bitter, resentful, and irritable struggling to hold our marriage together.

Jim also was experiencing emptiness and a sense of "where do we go from here"; but neither of us knew where to turn or how to deal with our circumstances. We tried many avenues--transcendental meditation, holistic medicine, the power of the mind--and still found no solace. None of these filled the void we both felt.

At the height of our success, we were invited to a dinner at the Fairmont Hotel in San Francisco. We really did not want to attend since the speaker was one of the men involved in "Watergate." Neither of us had an interest in hearing one more explanation of that scandal. After refusing the invitation several times, we finally acquiesced. We were surprised, however, to discover that the speech was related to "Watergate" only in that it had brought the speaker, Chuck Colson, into a life-changing relationship with God. Stunned by what was said, we silently left the room that night. Although we had both been in church on and off since childhood, we had never heard anything such as Mr. Colson related. He told how God had changed his heart, given him a new mind, a new perspective, and new goals that had carried him through his trials and given him hope and direction in life.

A few days after the dinner, our host for the evening gave us a copy of "Born Again," the book which Mr. Colson had written about his conversion experience. In his book, Chuck explained how, in frustration and despair, he had called out to Jesus Christ. He asked Christ to come into his life and deliver him from the misery he was experiencing. Somehow, although the circumstances were hardly the same, I understood the despair and longing that he described. I needed something but had been unable to find it. I wasn't even sure that God existed. I had bought into the idea that I could control my own destiny and by worldly success could become fulfilled. I thought that God was a good idea for those who needed Him, but I had never included myself in that category.

Upon finishing the book, I found myself asking God (if He really existed) to come into my life and take over. I had no control and needed something beyond my meager efforts to find the fulfillment I sought. I experienced no immediate sense of release or emotion. I had made a commitment to allow God to control my life and was ready for whatever came next.

A few months later we were invited to an "Executive Seminar" at <u>Campus Crusade for Christ</u> headquarters in Arrowhead Springs, California. We weren't sure what this seminar was all about, but we were attracted by the impressive list of successful men who were to be the keynote speakers. The first evening there, Dr. Bill Bright, founder and president of Campus Crusade, greeted us. He briefly explained that the one common strand bringing these top executives together was their relationship with Jesus Christ. He went on to tell us how we, too, could have this relationship with our Creator by merely confessing our sins and asking Christ to come into our lives. As we left the session, we were told to go to a quiet place, make a list of all our sins, ask God's forgiveness, and then destroy the list. This was symbolic of what Christ had done for us when He died on the cross. He took our sins from us, placed them upon Himself, and suffered the punishment of death for them. When Jim returned to the room that night, I knew something dramatic was happening to him. It came to a blessed conclusion the next morning when Dr. Bright invited us to his office. It was there that Jim prayed to receive Christ into his life.

Whereas my prayer had been a quiet surrender, Jim's was a stirring and exciting experience. He felt as though the weight of the world had been lifted from his shoulders and he was free. He was ready to "conquer hell with a water pistol." If fireworks and rockets go off in one's soul, they did in his.

I was delighted to have this common bond with Jim, and as the weekend continued, we learned some basics of this new relationship with God. We learned about prayer, confession of sin, and the ministry of the Holy Spirit. My Christian life began to take root as God taught me how to allow His Spirit to work in and through me.

When we left that weekend, Dr. Bright supplied books and tapes to aid us in the pursuit of this new aspect of our lives. We had lived in a spiritual desert for so long that we were dying of thirst for the things of God. For the first time, the Bible became real to us and we couldn't get enough. We were so hungry to learn about God and what He wanted in our lives that we attended nearly every Christian camp, conference, and event we could find. God began to teach us through His word and through some Godly men of our day how He intended for us to live.

I thought I could never be that woman with the **"gentle and quiet spirit that is precious in the sight of God"** as **I Peter 4** tells us. I wanted to have the patience and love and joy and gentleness described as the fruits of the

Spirit in Galatians. I never dreamed that all of this was mine merely by allowing God to live through me.

I first discovered that God really could work through me in everyday events of life when my children were arguing one day. My usual pattern was to jump in the middle, shout and rant, and make matters worse. This day, however, I asked God to help me solve the situation with grace and ease. God led me to handle it as I had prayed and the difficulty was easily resolved. God really is real!

We now had renewed hope for our marriage, our personal lives and the future. New life had sprung up within us. Our marriage began to be fashioned after God's pattern of selflessness, sacrifice, respect, and unconditional love for one another and for Him. Our relationship took on a new dimension. We wanted to live Godly lives and to be an example to others of His love.

As we began to rear our children together in the love of Christ, our mindset changed; money was no longer god, people were more important than projects, and our goals became more centered on what we could do for God and His kingdom. God trained us and changed our hearts in an incredibly short time. You see, He knew that our faith was about to be tested . . . , and it was indeed!

About two years into this new walk with Christ, Jim was indicted by the Federal government for fifteen counts of mail fraud connected with the firm he had helped to establish nine years previously. Our exuberant bubble began to explode.

How could this be happening to us? Why now? We had just dedicated our lives to serving the Lord! Had He not cleansed us and purified us? We were new creatures in Christ! Weren't we now living the kind of life that was pleasing to Him? Although these questions plagued us those first few weeks and months, God used this time to begin to teach us some of the most valuable lessons we had ever learned.

After two years of lawyers, hearings, delays, postponements, anxiety and frustration, the case finally came before the court. After six weeks of grueling testimony, witnesses, reporters, camera operators and curiosity seekers, the jury found Jim guilty of eight counts of mail fraud. The judge's sentence was 400 hours of community service, a $10,000 fine, and five years in prison.

Prison! People like us didn't go to prison. We had never even known anyone who had gone to prison. How could this be happening?

We had clung tenaciously to God and His word and had been upheld by His people throughout the process of the trial. Would He be enough to take us through the times ahead?

Jim's business had suffered under the strain of the past years, and all of our money had gone to pay for his defense. There was little left but the roof over our heads and the hope that God would see us through.

By the time Jim was to serve his sentence, the judge had reduced the time to one year in prison with four years' probation. This was great news since those who are sentenced to one year without incident usually serve only about four months.

We were confident that we could make it for four months on the money from Jim's company and with God's grace. Although the separation was difficult, we were heartened by the reduction of his sentence and the hope that we could carry on at home without my having to go to work, further disrupting our family.

During this period, God revealed to me **Philippians 4:19, ". . . and my God shall supply all your needs according to His riches in glory in Christ Jesus."** Apparently God wanted to use our difficult situation to teach me the truth of that scripture. Particularly during the separation from Jim, God proved to me that He is indeed sufficient to meet my every need.

He comforted me with His peace. Previously when Jim was away for a night, I would sleep lightly and uneasily, awaiting the unknown intruder who would enter our home noiselessly. Never, however, during this time did I spend a sleepless night, jumping at creaking floors or the wind about the house. I was wrapped in His peace and slept soundly and restfully in His care. He sheltered me under his wings.

He protected my children from the cruelty that could have come from their peers by providing them with supportive friends and Christian teachers. I recently learned that my daughter's third-grade teacher would hold my daughter in her lap and let her cry privately when she was overcome by emotions.

He gave me physical strength to meet the demands of my family of five. In addition to studying and preparing lessons for my Bible Study Fellowship class of 150, I had to do laundry, cook six toteable meals, and prepare for the ten-hour drive to the prison each weekend.

When I was overwhelmed by the seeming impossibility of it all, God sent precious friends to my rescue. The discussion leaders in my Bible Study class provided the six meals for us to take to the prison during our long days of visiting. This not only freed me from a tremendous amount of planning, shopping, and cooking but also served to help us out financially.

God met our financial needs when our funds ran out halfway through Jim's sentence. People, moved by God, gave--and gave abundantly! When my husband's partner called to tell me our funds were depleted, my first thought was that I would have to get a job. We felt strongly that God did not want me to work. It was important that our home be as normal as possible for the few months Jim would be incarcerated. I was confused and concerned but had no idea how I would otherwise pay the outstanding bills and provide for our material needs. I talked with my Bible study class administrator the next day and asked her to pray with me about finding a new leader; I was sure I would be joining the work force. When I arrived home that night, I found on the doorstep an envelope containing a $1,000 check. Exactly the amount I needed to pay all our bills. Again, God showed me that He had the resources to care for us. I was beginning to learn that God wanted me to live by faith, not by sight.

     For the remainder of our separation, God continued to sustain us through the generosity of people moved by God to share their riches with us. Another day when money was scarce, a friend slipped something in my pocket. She said she had been putting a few dollars away here and there and felt that God wanted her to share her "stash" with me. I went home that day $100 richer and yet again amazed by our gracious Heavenly Father. Often, as I opened my mail, I would find a letter with a cashier's check from an unknown source.

God drew us closer as a family and began to heal and restore the girls' relationship with their father as they spent uninterrupted hours visiting, playing games, walking and talking together at the prison. At last, they had their father's undivided attention.

Our God supplies--and supplies richly! We made it through this difficult time and were better off for the experience.

After Jim's return, there was nothing left of his business in California. The best prospect of starting over came from an acquaintance in Oklahoma. We packed our belongings, bid a sad farewell to our dear friends in California, and set out to begin again.

We found a wonderful church and community. Jim began to regain financial stability, and we began to rebuild our broken lives. For about a year we were able to restore our souls and regain our strength. Then, quite unexpectedly, the IRS ran a "sting" operation on this new company to entrap one of the principals suspected of criminal activity. My worst fears were realized when Jim was drawn into the situation, and we found ourselves back in court facing probation violation charges.

Have you ever been sick all over when you are struck with hard news? That was my reaction as I walked into the Federal Building for our second trial. All the difficult emotions came flooding back. These halls represented four years of hurt and pain that I thought were finally behind us. Our finances were none too strong, we were in a new community, we were trying to rebuild our lives, and now this! To add to our crisis, other things began to look bleak as well.

It was just two weeks before Christmas. We had been waiting for a business transaction to be signed that would see us through the holidays and enable us to buy gifts for the family. Monday, while driving to school to pick up one of my daughters, I heard a terrible sound coming from the car's engine. I drove immediately to the garage where I discovered that I had "thrown a rod" and would be unable to drive the car unless the engine was completely rebuilt. I had no money to do that, so we were without our second vehicle. Tuesday, Jim was involved in an accident that put our primary mode of transportation out of commission. Wednesday, the business transaction we were counting on fell apart, and we were facing Christmas with literally no funds. We heard Thursday that Jim would have to face charges and stand trial again. What a devastating week! Our heads were reeling from all that had taken place. We weren't sure how to go on but again sought God's intervention.

Friday of that same week God reminded us once more that He is our provider and sustainer. It began when our oldest daughter came home from visiting a friend who lived with her grandmother. The Gramma, whom we had never met, had noticed that Katie's coat was old and worn. That night, we received a call from Gramma who said she wanted to buy a new coat for Katie for Christmas. We were stunned, but delighted and grateful. She explained that her granddaughter had told her about Katie's three sisters and she didn't think it fair to give to one without giving something to the others. She sent us four checks for $100 to buy gifts for each girl, and a coat for Katie.

On Sunday, a young man from our church called Jim. He had just bought a new car, and God had put it upon his heart to give us his old one. That afternoon he brought the car which was to become our mainstay for years to come. The same day, another friend from church had heard about our accident and brought his van for us to use until our first car could be repaired.

The next evening we attended a Christmas gathering of leaders of a Bible Study Fellowship class I had been teaching. They had taken an offering to purchase a Christmas gift for us but felt it wiser just to give us the money. We left there with a paper sack filled with bills and coins. At home, we all joined in to count the money, and to our amazement, found $500. Bills could be paid and the Christmas lights could continue to shine.

Thursday of the next week, I found boxes and boxes of food on my kitchen counters. The church had brought a "Christmas Basket," with turkey, dressing, pumpkin pie and several meals of canned goods. That night Jim announced that the failed transaction had been "resurrected." We could see hope for January. Friday, two unexpected checks appeared in our mailbox.

Don't ever let anyone tell you that the Christian life is dull. God is full of surprises. Even in the bleakest times, He is sufficient. He wanted us to be continually reminded of that sufficiency as we approached the time of our second trial.

Our church friends packed the courtroom on the day of sentencing. Many had testified and written letters in defense of Jim's character, but the judge showed no mercy. He revoked Jim's probation and sentenced him to prison to serve the remainder of his three plus years' probation.

As Jim was shackled and led from the courtroom, my heart broke. Our children, teenagers now, were crushed. Our 14-year-old sobbed uncontrollably as our friends tried to comfort her.

We returned home and somehow began to adjust to the reality of our situation. The first days were spent in a daze. For the first time in my life, I was emotionally drained to the point of depression. Sin has devastating consequences that must always be faced, and it affects so many innocent people.

Satan plagued me with thoughts of people who had been hurt by Jim's actions. So many stood by us, yet many just couldn't understand what had happened and turned away. The pain of rejection, real or imagined, is equally agonizing. We were blessed with wonderfully supportive and loving families, who, although wounded and humiliated by our circumstances, continued to love and encourage us. They endured the hardships with and for us, yet never judged, condemned, or spoke a disparaging word. They were true examples and constant reminders of God's unconditional love for His children.

I continued going to church, praying, and studying God's Word even though the song had gone from my heart and I couldn't see God's hand in sending Jim back to prison. Truly, we must trust God's heart when we can't trace His hand.

One evening, at a church Bible study on the book of James, God quite unexpectedly lifted the veil. As Christians, we had learned to thank God in all circumstances as instructed in Philippians and had paid lip service to **James 1:2,** which instructs us to **"consider it all joy, my brethren, when you encounter various trials . . . ."** Somehow I had missed the last part of that exhortation. We read on to verses **3** and **4, ". . . knowing that the testing of your faith produces endurance. And let endurance have its perfect result, that you may be perfect and complete, lacking in nothing."** A light suddenly came on, and I was lifted out of my despair and set free! Now I knew God's purpose in allowing these circumstances. It was the very answer to my heart's desire: "to be perfect and complete, lacking in nothing." That's what God had in mind for me and my family. How could anyone dispute that? God had a purpose for which I was to be the benefactor.

From that time on, God gave me peace and joy in our circumstances. I learned to live one day at a time and watched as God repeatedly proved Himself in miraculous ways. I saw Him work in the lives of our four precious daughters, building character and faith.

Our oldest daughter was a freshman at the University of Oklahoma. A dear family friend provided her, and subsequently our next two children, with a grant to cover tuition. This grant, along with the jobs she held all during college, completely provided for her education. A Phi Beta Kappa, she graduated first in her major. Our second daughter, as a junior in high school, worked for her expense money. When she graduated from high school, Jim was granted a furlough to attend. (This was the first furlough granted at that institution.) Her college expenses were supplemented by scholarships. In addition she received love offerings while singing with a contemporary Christian quartet. She graduated Cum Laude, and today still sings with "Point of Grace," sharing God's love across the country.

Our third daughter, while a freshman in high school, was also provided with a good job that helped sustain us during those difficult days. She worked selflessly after school and on weekends yet continued to be active in high school and youth group activities.

The "baby" was a seventh grader and a joy to us all. When we first arrived in Oklahoma, she attended a little country school where she was labeled the "rich" kid from California. After the trial, we were forced to give up our home in the country and move to a small rental house in the city. We continued the 25-minute drive to the country so she could complete her year there. Each day as we drove, she read aloud from the book of Proverbs. We prayed for her to be able, with God's grace, to withstand the ostracism she was experiencing. By the end of the year, she had won the respect and affection of her peers and her teachers.

Probably the most vivid description of the support we received came one night to our 17-year-old. She awakened me saying that she had dreamed we were all at home and realized that a burglar with a knife was outside our house trying to break in. We ran to the doors and windows to check the locks. As we looked outside, there were all our precious friends surrounding the house and forming a chain of protection about us. God is our protector!

Another area of provision came from Jim's Air Force Academy classmates. Many of these men were still serving in the Air Force and were now colonels and generals. They were men of stature who knew how to "take control." I received many calls of encouragement from these good friends. One day a letter arrived explaining a plan to help us. A letter was being circulated to their classmates to establish a fund for our attorneys' fees. They were concerned about our representation and, with my consent, found new counsel. Their support was a blessing in an area we could not otherwise have handled.

It had been twenty years since I had been a part of the work force. I had no marketable skills. My teaching credentials had long since expired, and I didn't type. I had no idea where to begin, yet as always God supplied.

The first job He provided me was with an attorney from our church, who asked me to open his new office. This was a true blessing to me. Although I couldn't teach school or type, God had given me the gift of organization and was now allowing me to use that gift for our support. After this office was established, I was approached by the church staff to work in the church office. I quickly accepted and spent the next four years happily serving as receptionist and secretary to the Youth and Music ministers. Again, God knew what I needed. I was surrounded by wonderful Christian people who were aware of my circumstances and sympathetic to my special needs. Not only was I ministered to, but God allowed me to minister for Him. As time went on, I received invitations to give my testimony and lead Bible studies for the hurting and wounded. Just when I thought God had put me "on the shelf," He began to use my experiences to comfort others. **(II Corinthians 1:3-4)**

We were continually amazed at the many ways in which God provided for us. Often when cash was low, I would receive those mysterious checks in the mail or donations made to us through the church. One of the most creative ways God worked began one day when I received a letter from the telephone company. The letter informed me that I had been paying $4 a month for a service I had not received, but they would rectify the error by installing the service. I immediately called the company and told them I hadn't missed the service and didn't care to have it installed. The amazed employee then asked if perhaps I would prefer to have the money reimbursed. I said that I would but certainly I didn't expect much reimbursement at $4 a month. The clerk added the overcharges, which had been billed on both of our phone lines for over four years, and the total was approximately $400. God had given me a little savings account that I never knew I had; then He gave me the money when I needed it most. What a creative Lord!

Just as He proved Himself a faithful provider for us in the "free world," He also began a mighty work in Jim's life. He helped Jim to realize his guilt, helplessness, and need of total surrender to Christ and His authority. Though Jim was unable to do anything more than give encouragement to us at home, God showed him that He had a plan for him in every circumstance of life, even prison. He used Jim and others to bring a full-scale revival to that prison. Our lives were uniquely and wonderfully blessed as we saw God work in Jim and in those around him. Our church family donated books to provide a Christian library for the prison; they organized and participated in softball games at the facility. They sang, preached, and led chapel services and Bible studies. They sent cards and letters, befriended the friendless, and brought hope to the hopeless. They bought laughter and joy into the lives of the inmates, and through these acts of love, many prisoners came to a saving knowledge of Jesus Christ.

It has been nearly six years since Jim was restored to our family. So many of our hearts' desires have been granted in that time. A good job awaited Jim when he was released. I remained at the church for a time until we could open our own businesses and work side by side. We have seen three of our four children graduate from college and marry Godly men of faith. We watched breathlessly as God spared our first grandchild who was born with a serious heart condition. He has enabled us to provide a college education for our youngest, who, as well as winning scholarships and honors at Baylor University, helps by working 20 hours a week. What undeserved blessings God reserves for his children. It's called GRACE!

In February of 1994, God met another of our hearts' desires. Since becoming Christians, we had a growing desire to serve God in some type of ministry. What that would be, we did not know. When our youngest went to college, God began opening doors for us. Suddenly, Christian organizations were inviting us to serve with them in bringing Christ into the lives of others. One of those organizations, the Bill Glass Ministries, asked Jim to direct their Prison Ministry Department. This was the one place I had no desire to serve--in the prisons! I wanted to get as far away from that part of our lives as possible. I did, however, say I would pray about it; and God, in His wisdom, miraculously changed my heart. We were uniquely qualified to minister to those behind bars, and God was not going to waste our experience.

We left our precious friends and church family to move to the headquarters near Dallas, Texas. Since then, we have embarked on one of the most challenging and rewarding phases of our lives. We bring hundreds of volunteer counselors into the prisons of America to share the life-changing message of the Good News of Jesus Christ to those without hope, help or purpose.

As you can see, our lives have not been what we anticipated 30 years ago as we stood at that altar thinking we could meet each other's needs and that the riches of the world would make us happy and fulfilled. We wouldn't, however, trade anything for the experiences we have had. God taught us that we are enriched and matured through the trials of life so that we may find true fulfillment, which comes only from above. We have been from riches . . . to rags . . . to God's riches, and **WE ARE BLESSED!**

Bonnie Lang is the mother of four beautiful girls. Bonnie and her husband Jim are working full time for the Bill Glass ministries out of Cedar Hill, TX. They are currently heading up the Bill Glass Prison Ministry.

Margolyn Woods

The 1972 Pasadena Tournament of Roses Queen is . . .

It was early morning as we stood on the steps of the Wrigley Mansion in Pasadena, California. All seven of us stood smiling at a sea of cameras. I tried to get a glimpse of Linda out of the corner of my eyes. Everyone knew that Linda would be the Queen; she was so poised and beautiful.

Margolyn Johnson, a freshman attending Pasadena City College from Arcadia, California.

"What did he say?" For a second I hesitated, not knowing for sure that I had heard what I heard. Then I felt a nudge forward from Julie. Oh my gosh! It's me!! I looked over the audience and realized they were clapping for me! I saw my mom and dad with tears in their eyes, and I smiled at them as I stepped forward to the microphone.

Someone thrust a beautiful bouquet of roses in my arms and someone else turned me toward the TV cameras.

A young man from a local TV station came up to me as the applause subsided. "Congratulations on being the

83rd Tournament of Roses Queen, Margolyn. Can you tell us what winning the title means to you?"

I remember the roses shaking as I wiped tears from my cheeks. "Thank you," I said. "This is so exciting! Since moving to California, I have watched the Rose Parade, and like all little girls who grow up in this area, I dreamed of being the Queen one day. This is going to be a tremendous year for me, and I am already extremely grateful to see the joy this has brought my parents."

I meant it, too. I had enjoyed a wonderful childhood with two loving parents, a brother and a sister. There were music lessons, campfire girls, community and church activities, and family vacations--a childhood full of lovely, loving memories.

Now all of a sudden I was caught up in a whole new world of adventure and excitement.

After the press conference, Mom and Dad took me home to get ready for my first public appearance that evening as "Queen." I'll never forget that car ride home as my folks and I talked a hundred miles an hour anticipating the exciting events of the coming months! When we turned the corner to our street, we saw all of the cars. Who would ever have dreamed that so many people would come by our home to offer their congratulations! And that was only the beginning!! When the pictures hit the newspapers, we received cards, letters, phone calls, and telegrams from all over the United States and Canada.

The first few weeks were filled with fittings for the many clothes, hairdresser appointments, briefings on questions I may be asked, and homework!

I spent the next twelve months promoting the Tournament of Roses. There were appearances every day, sometimes in as many as five different places a day. Many appearances were with the Grand Marshall of the parade, Mr. Lawrence Welk. This wonderful man shared my thrill at being chosen by the Tournament of Roses. What a treat to see how he was respected at every event we attended, truly, one of God's "Gentlemen."

I'll never forget my very first television appearance. Mr. Welk invited me to be his guest on the New Year's Eve television broadcast of "The Lawrence Welk Show." National television!! I was <u>so</u> nervous. Then on <u>live</u> television, he offered to teach me to polka! Me, with two left feet!! I had been fortunate to get a tape of the show. We still have a good laugh because most of the segment was shot from our waists up, so as not to show my feet!

Calls began for me to appear on other television shows, such as the Bob Hope Christmas Show, the Andy Williams Christmas Special, the Flip Wilson Show, the Carol Burnett Show, Hollywood Squares and College Bowl. I was even asked to do the very first television commercial for a brand new product, the Polaroid Camera.

I was treated like a star with all the trimmings: a new wardrobe, hairdressers, limousine drivers, and wonderful gifts. Loving every minute, I basked in all the glory. I loved "show business" and, although I was a music major in college, I quickly decided that I wanted a career in the limelight.

During that year I had many other personal appearance requests, from opening Expo in Montreal,

Canada, to helping promote the Armed Forces. I was asked to judge beauty pageants and to speak to different clubs, churches and organizations. These were wonderful opportunities to promote the Tournament of Roses Association and to share with everyone how much fun I was having.

It was after one of these speaking engagements that a young man came up to me and said, "Thank you so much for sharing with us tonight. It was great to hear all about the Tournament activities, but I was just wondering if you have ever asked Jesus Christ to be the Lord and Savior of your life?"

I don't recall exactly what I said to the young man, but I remember thinking that he must be one of those "Jesus freaks" I had heard about. He made me feel uncomfortable. I recall getting out of the situation gracefully; his words, however, would come back to me many years later.

The parade was wonderful . . . such excitement and the fulfillment of so many dreams! I thought I had the world by the tail and was on my way to stardom!

One day near the end of my reign, a representative from Western Airlines asked me if I would be interested in coming to work for them. He said they were looking for a flight attendant who would also help them with public relations assignments. What a great job! I immediately jumped on the offer and spent a magnificent two years with Western Airlines. However, the acting bug had bitten, and I soon left the airlines to start the rounds of interviews for movies and television shows and commercials.

I had an incredibly lucky start in the entertainment industry. At one point I had three national commercials on the air simultaneously and a two-year contract with Rose Milk Skin Care products.

I was very young and foolish, however. I remember interviewing for a national commercial spot in which the actress had to know how to jet-ski. Wanting the job, I lied and told them I could trick ski. The job was mine, but I spent almost as much as I made paying someone to teach me (in four days) how to jet ski off a ramp.

I loved acting though and nothing seemed to discourage me. I was always hoping to get the <u>next</u> job-- the one that looked so wonderful. I was on my way and financially stable.

At a dinner party one evening I met a famous film producer. He lived in the limelight and in the fast lane; he had been married to Raquel Welch (launched her career); and now he was paying attention to me!

For our first date he invited me to his home for lunch. I remember driving around the Hollywood Hills and admiring the homes. Pulling up to his rambling hilltop home, I really thought I had "arrived."

After an exciting year of dating, we were married in a star-studded ceremony. Everyone from Tony Curtis to Hugh Hefner attended. Our reception was held in the home of a famous composer with the press clamoring to take photos.

Our life was full of parties and premieres! Part of the year we spent in London, England, and part in Beverly Hills, California. An exhilarating, glorious new life was opened to me. It was a life where people quoted us and where the press made up stories about us; where people were nice to us and then talked about us behind our backs. Hooray for Hollywood!

The marriage came with two stepchildren who were about as excited at having a new stepmother as I was at having stepchildren.

Several years passed. With my husband away making films, often for months at a time, I was left at home to play mom to two teenagers. We began to grow apart.

The parties and the people weren't nearly so exciting anymore. In fact, the whole "show business" scene became rather superficial to me. Most important was that you were invited to the right parties and with whom you were seen! I saw less and less of my husband, and eventually we divorced.

Ready to concentrate on my career again, I moved into a nearby condo. It was lonely at first and I knew that something was missing from my life. I was sure that if I could find a husband <u>out of show-business,</u> I would be happy.

About a year and "400" blind dates later, I got a phone call from my good friend Mark. A friend was visiting from out of town, and Mark asked if I would like to meet them for lunch. He went on to say that his friend was attractive, successful, and <u>out of show-business</u>. I couldn't help wondering if this might be the one.

Arriving fashionably ten minutes late to make my entrance to the restaurant in Beverly Hills, I knew at once this man had potential. He was attractive and had a great smile. He wore jeans, with a huge silver belt buckle, and cowboy boots. When he spoke, I noticed his strong Oklahoma accent. This man really stood out in Beverly Hills!

From the minute we were introduced, Roy Woods and I felt comfortable with each other. During lunch, he asked me to dinner that evening. Unfortunately, I was shooting an episode of a show called "Vegas" in Las Vegas and had to leave that afternoon. I had to tell Roy no, but he promised to call the next time he was in Los Angeles.

All the way to Las Vegas, I felt like kicking myself. How could this happen? When I finally find a fabulous guy, he is GU (<u>G</u>eographically <u>U</u>ndesirable). Upon arrival in Las Vegas, I found my room filled with flowers and a note attached saying, *Until next time! Roy.*

I thought, "Oh my gosh, not only is he cute, polite, and out of show-business . . . , he's romantic!"

We set a date the following month when he would be back in Los Angeles. The month went by so slowly. I could hardly concentrate on anything. Was I reading more into this than there was?

When he called to confirm the date, he asked me to meet his plane. You can imagine my surprise when I realized that he meant "his" plane.

I thought, "Oh my gosh, not only is he cute, polite, out of show-business, and romantic . . . , he's rich!!"

I must have changed clothes four times before I left for the airport that evening. I stood on the tarmac as his

Margolyn Woods

plane glided over me--not a small private plane, but a Lockeed Jet-Star, with bright blue and red racing stripes. I remember thinking, "I could get used to this kind of life."

After only a few dates, I knew that he was the one for me. Roy was charming and had some of that old-fashioned chivalry not found much in Beverly Hills! He wanted to settle down, to have children, and to attend church. He was successful, and . . . he was out of show-business! So, after three short weeks, we eloped.

I hadn't planned to elope, but Roy, a professional race car driver, was leaving to race at Le Mans, France, and it sounded so romantic to run off and elope!

I tried to find my folks to let them know, but they were vacationing in Europe and I couldn't locate them. I wondered what they would think about all of this. I had always been close to them, and they had been really supportive and helpful during my divorce. It seemed odd not to have them as a part of my marriage plans.

We flew to Las Vegas with my best friend and her husband, Roy's sister and her husband. We were married on

the strip in a bright pink chapel with a neon sign flashing
"All Checks O.K." It was not exactly the wedding I had
hoped for but I felt great. I had a wonderful husband, and I
knew this time that it was forever. Our honeymoon in the
south of France was filled with wonderful hotels, incredible
meals, limousines, and shopping.

We finally located my parents, and I'll never forget
my mom's comment. After a very long pause she said, "Well
dear, you must really be in love if you are going to move to
Oklahoma. We wish you all the best." And certainly we had
the "best." I had heard of the term born with a "silver"
spoon in one's mouth, but his was "gold."

I quit show-business and moved to Oklahoma City
where life seemed perfect. Our home was a beautiful estate
called "Out of Bounds." This was a home that could easily
seat 50 in the living room. We had a waterfall in the house
and a concert grand piano sitting in the window overlooking
the 9th hole of the Oklahoma City Golf and Country Club.
The grounds had a beautiful lake stocked with a variety of
fish and a sunken tennis court. The six-car garage housed a

Ferarri, a Lamborghini, a Mercedes, and a Jaguar. Since there was a full staff, my days consisted only of choosing the daily menus, doing a little volunteer work, and shopping.

For a while everything was wonderful. Our lives were filled with benefits--planes, wonderful trips--and filled with lots of love. It was a lifestyle that I had only read about. Roy thought nothing of ordering the plane to take us to dinner in Dallas or a foursome of golfers to another city if it was raining in Oklahoma City.

This marriage also came with two stepchildren, 13 and 15 years old, two girls whom I'd never met and who were totally shocked at their dad's remarriage. Each responded differently. After Bekki would leave from a visit with us, every picture of me in the house would be missing. Robyn was much more subtle. She would compliment me on something I was wearing, then the next time I planned to wear it, it would be gone.

After several exciting yet tiring years on the race-car circuit, I was ready to settle down. I asked Roy to give up racing, and he said, "Someday, sure, but not now!" When I asked him about having children, he said the same thing. When I asked him about going to church with me on Sunday, he would say, "On my golf day?" When I asked him about coming home at six to have dinner with me, he said, "Hey, you're lucky to have me!"

Indeed! I thought that I had done the big favor; after all, I had quit show-business and moved to <u>Oklahoma City!</u> On the outside, it must have looked like I had everything, but I wasn't very happy. I was lonely. I didn't know many people in Oklahoma City, and I recognized the signs of a marriage in trouble. I had been there before.

One family whom I had met in Oklahoma City was the Hartzogs, a wonderful family with seven children but who always seemed to have time for me. While Roy was off on the race car circuit or playing golf, they took me to church on Sundays and Gretchen took me to the Christian Women's Club. It was Gretchen that I turned to and cried on her shoulder for hours. She listened to me and then asked me that same question I had heard so many years before,

"Margolyn have you ever asked Jesus to be your Lord and Savior?"

She went on to tell me that God loves me and desires for me to be close to Him. All of us have sinned and fallen short of the glory of God, but God sent His son Jesus to die for our sins. And although He died, He was resurrected on the third day and He lives at the right hand of the Father today.

She referred to the words of Jesus in **John 14:6, "I am the way, the truth, and the life; no one comes to the Father but through me."** And, Jesus said, **"Behold I stand at the door and knock; if anyone hears my voice and opens the door, I will come in to him."**

She explained that to be a Christian I must ask Jesus to come into my life. I couldn't believe what I was hearing. I thought I was a Christian. I had grown up in church, sung in the choir, and attended youth groups; but I had never heard anyone explain the Gospel to me as Gretchen explained it to me that day.

She asked me if I wanted to invite Jesus to come in and take control of my life. Well, my life surely wasn't working the way I was handling it. I recognized that I had truly never made God a part of my life, so I prayed a prayer with her that day that went something like this:

Dear Lord, I need you. Thank you for dying for me. I open the door of my heart and receive you as my Savior and Lord. Thank you for forgiving my sins and for giving me the gift of eternal life. Please take control of my life and make me into the kind of person that you would have me be. In Jesus' name I pray. Amen.

For me, it was as if a light came on in my life. I now knew why I was always searching, why I felt so empty, and why I looked to people and things to make me happy. I had a void in my life that only Jesus could fill.

I had depended on money, people, and accomplishments to make me happy, but they never truly did. You know, many people are just like me. They think, "Oh, when I get that raise or when we get to go on that vacation, or when the kids are just a little bit older or when

I retire, then I'll be happy. They spend their whole lives waiting for happiness or thinking that it will be around the next corner, when they could have had it all along.

I feel really lucky because I have had some of those "things" and have come to know from experiences that "things" don't bring true happiness. Oh sure, you feel good for the moment or for a little while, but it's not true happiness, and it's not lasting.

I needed the Lord to be the center of my life, for He has a definite plan and purpose for me, Margolyn; and simply by surrendering to Him, I have the promise of eternal life.

I had, of course, heard the term "unequally yoked," but now I understood it better. As I grew closer to the Lord through fellowship, Bible study, church and prayer, Roy moved further and further away from me. Finally, because of his infidelity, I felt I had to leave him. Nobody knows the feelings invoked by infidelity until one goes through it. I just wanted to get as far away from Roy as I could.

I didn't want to stay in Oklahoma, and I surely didn't want to go back to the Hollywood scene. I moved to Colorado where, with the help of friends, I began to put my life back together. I felt like such a failure. I had been given what most people only dream about in their lives, but I could not make it work. I was incredibly hurt and lonely. I went to bed each night with an ache inside. My only comfort came through prayer.

Every night I prayed that Roy might find the peace and love that I had found with Jesus. I prayed that God would deliver Roy from his worldly ways and that he would find himself surrounded by Christians! I never prayed, however, that he would come back to me. The pain was just too intense.

It is true that time does help to heal our hurts. New friends and a busy life helped diminish much of the aching. I found a church home and a peace that comes only from knowing our Lord Jesus Christ.

Roy started calling me; he was sorry and he missed me. At first, his voice brought back all of those awful feelings, but I loved him and it didn't take long to realize that I looked forward to his calls. Somehow, there was safety in distance, and we could share feelings.

Then one day, over a year later, Roy knocked at my door, a suitcase in hand, wanting to start over. The divorce had gone through (in Oklahoma you can be divorced in about two minutes), but I let him move back in and things were wonderful for a while. I thought we had a good chance of working things out because we were starting fresh in a new town. I felt secure with him, and I thought he was happy in Colorado. He wasn't. The world's "fast-lane" still had a hold on Roy. One day I came home to a note telling me that he had left. I was shattered, and a month later, I found out I was pregnant!

I had wanted children all of my life. Now after two failed marriages, I was 31 years old, single, and pregnant! I was devastated! I had heard of teenagers "making a mistake" and getting pregnant, but I had never heard of someone my age making that mistake. What was I going to do? Who could I even tell? What had I done?

I felt differently from the moment I thought I might
be pregnant. I had taken a home pregnancy test, but I was
certain even before I took the test. It seemed as if the whole
world was moving at a fast speed but my life had come to a
halt. How could this be happening to me? After many tears,
I fell to my knees, prayed for forgiveness, and asked that
God would stay close and help me through this.

For the first two months, I simply felt sorry for
myself. Then God put it on my heart that a baby was
growing inside me. I stopped and looked at every baby.
Was my baby a boy or a girl? What would my baby look
like? So many questions.

I decided to go to a doctor for a checkup. I almost
turned around and left when I saw all of the happy expecting
mothers in the waiting room. But I didn't. I filled out forms
instead--forms that labeled me as a single mother. My
emotions were on edge as the doctor examined me. Smiling,
he pronounced a healthy baby growing inside of me, . . . and
then the tears came. After consoling me, he asked if I would
like to see my baby on ultrasound. He must have spent

twenty more minutes with me, even with a waiting room full of patients. Only another mother knows the joy that comes from hearing the baby's heartbeat for the first time and watching the baby on the ultrasound screen.

I left the doctor's office a new woman. I decided to sell my home and move to Maui, where Roy and I shared a condo in the divorce. I found a wonderful church. I didn't "show" much and somehow it just seemed difficult to share what I was going through with casual acquaintances. So, I stayed mostly to myself until one Sunday when I noticed in our church bulletin that a childbirth class was being held.

I arrived at the home where the class was to take place and noticed that both pastors and their wives were there. They may have been shocked to see me, but all I remember is their hugs and warmth as I entered. We sat in a semicircle on the floor as introductions were made and we shared why we wanted to take the Bradley Method of Childbirth. By the time my turn came, the tears were flowing. I don't recall exactly what I said, but I do remember the love and encouragement I felt from this wonderful group of Christian couples.

For the next couple of months, I was invited to homes for dinner, included in birthdays, and involved in a Bible study. I looked forward to childbirth classes and even had several people offer to help me at delivery time.

Wouldn't you know! About five months later there was another knock at the door, and again it was Roy. This time he really had worked through his worldly problems and was ready to start over. I was skeptical. Would he leave me again? Could I love him fully? Could I ever trust him?

Roy went to church with me and attended the childbirth classes. Boy, were those Christian guys ever ready for him! They played golf and tennis with him, and they invited us to their homes. For the first time in our relationship, we spent a great deal of time with couples who loved the Lord. We had fun, whether it was playing a board game or just visiting at a pot luck dinner. Roy saw that these men had a "high" in their lives without drugs or expensive toys, and he respected their lifestyles, their relationships, and the way they treated their families.

Roy continued to attend church with me. One day when Pastor Craig asked if there were those who would like to give their lives to Christ, Roy, in tears, asked Jesus into his life. We were married shortly afterwards--after counseling and before the birth of our precious daughter Taryn.

Isn't it a miracle how God can heal a marriage! If anyone had told me that I would forgive Roy and fall in love with him all over again, I would have never believed it. Now I know that all things are possible through Christ for those who love Him and are called according to His purpose.

We have a wonderful marriage because our lives are centered on the Lord. By that I mean that we truly love our Lord Jesus Christ and both want to be like Him and to be in His will. Our marriage is not perfect or without problems or arguments. In fact, any of you living near Oklahoma may have heard my reaction when he showed up with a motorcycle this past summer! But we work out our

problems with the Lord's help.   As admonished in
Ephesians, we try not to let the sun set on our anger. We
also try to be good stewards of the blessings God has given
us. We grow in the Lord through fellowship with other
Christians, our church, and through Bible study and prayer.
We've been married 16 years, and the Lord has blessed us
with identical twin boys, now 9 years old. (Taryn is 11 years
old.) And remember those two stepdaughters I was so at
odds with? Today they are an integral part of our lives,
complete with a wonderful son-in-law and a beautiful
granddaughter, Megan, 2 years old.

      We moved from Hawaii to a farm in Oklahoma.
The farm has proven to be a great blessing for us. Not only
has it brought us closer together as a family but it has truly
given us a chance to know God better.

      We are raising sheep. Did you know that every
sheep is different (just like us)? I can tell you which one of
my sheep is greedy or which one is shy or ornery. I think of
all the times that God calls us His sheep.   He doesn't see us

as a flock; He sees us as individuals and desires for us to be close to Him.

My life is complete. I no longer feel empty and no longer look for worldly things to make me happy. They never really did.

I start every day in prayer with God. I begin with praise and thanksgiving for all His blessings, then I ask forgiveness for anything I may have done in thought, word, or deed that was not pleasing to Him. I ask God to use me each day to encourage someone who feels discouraged, give hope to someone who feels hopeless, love someone who feels unloved, listen to someone who needs a friend, pray for those who need prayer, and in all things share Christ.

I cling to a special scripture: **"This is the day that the Lord has made and I will rejoice and be glad in it!"** To me it means to delight in each day. Or as my kids say, "Mom is making memories." I try to get the most out of every day--memorizing the sound of my daughter's laughter or the feeling of holding my little boy's pudgy hands. These times pass so quickly with our children.

Our priorities have completely changed. Our life goal is to have all our family and friends walking with the Lord, assured of eternal life with Christ. It is a humbling responsibility, but I believe as it says in the Bible, all things are possible through Christ Jesus, for He truly is the way, the truth, and the life.

A few years ago I lost a dear friend in a tragic accident. While getting out of the bathtub, she stepped on the cord to her hair dryer and was electrocuted. She was a true gift in my life, a godly mother of four boys, and a gifted Bible teacher. On the morning we heard that Marilyn had died, I was devastated! But I believe, as it says in the Bible, that our days are numbered in the Book of Life, and although we were shocked at the news of Marilyn's passing, I know Heaven was rejoicing that morning saying, "Marilyn is home!"

You see, none of us know when our number is up. So, if you have never asked Jesus into your life, I'm writing this today to encourage you to see what a difference Jesus can make. I know because He <u>is</u> my life.

Margolyn Woods

If you'd like to invite Jesus to be your Lord and Savior, pray a prayer something like the one I prayed with Gretchen those years ago:

Dear Lord, I need you. Thank you for dying for my sins. Thank you for forgiving my sins and for your promise of eternal life! I open the door of my heart and ask you to come in as my Savior and Lord. Please make me into the kind of person you would have me be. In your precious name, Jesus, I pray. Amen.

Margolyn Woods (a former Rose Bowl Queen and actress) lives on a farm in Oklahoma with her husband Roy and three of their five children. Margolyn, the author of three other books, is active on the Christian Speakers Circuit.

Pat Breckenridge

I believe that every woman has her personal, private box of memories in which she has tucked the experiences of times past. Some of them are warm and wonderful; others are tinged with pain and sadness. In the following pages, I will share some of my memories, which are probably not very different from yours.

One of my earliest memories was the first day of school. Do you remember that day? I even recall what I wore. My mother had taken me to the big town of Enid, Oklahoma, and bought me five new dresses. I felt like the richest girl in the world. I suppose, even at that young age, I thought if I wore a dress that made me feel pretty, I would have more confidence. So I chose a green and white checkered dress with a peter-pan collar and a big bow at the waist. My mother helped me into the dress, tied the bow, and gave me an approving look. In a very grown-up tone, I told her, "Now, Mother, don't come to the bus with me." (I wanted those older kids to think that I was big enough to get on the bus by myself.)

My eyes peered out the farmhouse window, watching for the enormous yellow school bus that would swallow me up and carry me into a brand new world. No doubt my mother, with tears running down her cheeks, stood at the kitchen window watching me, for she knew that things would never be quite the same.

Finally, the bus arrived. With shoulders stretched tall and back straight, I marched out trying to look very confident. I don't recall details about the rest of the day, but I do remember exactly how I felt. Inside that green and white school dress was a scared little girl. Her heart was beating very fast, her legs were shaking, and her palms were sweating. The little girl wondered how she would make it through this frightening new experience.

While growing up, my parents took me to church every time the doors were opened. At a very young age, I knew who the person of Jesus Christ was. I knew that He was born in a manger to Mary, a virgin. He grew up working in his father's carpenter shop. He lived on this earth as we do, breathing this air, walking, and talking. He had a three-year ministry with men called disciples, and He performed many miracles. When He was 33 years old, some evil men had nailed His hands and feet to an old wooden cross, and He died there for our sins.

It seemed that I had always loved Jesus, and I wanted Him to love me, too! It seemed that the only way He would love me would be for me to be very, very good. Never did a little girl try to be so good! However, I became frustrated in my attempts because I could never be as good as I thought I needed to be. I would appear to be perfect on the outside, but on the inside there were thoughts and attitudes that wouldn't be pleasing to God. As hard as I tried, I just couldn't seem to control them!

One year Brother James came to my church to lead a series of services. As I listened to him talk, I began to think that he knew all about me. He said according to the Bible, **"All have sinned and fallen short of the glory of God."** He put it in language I understood and said it meant that no one is perfect. I breathed a sigh of relief. At least I wasn't the only one with this problem. He went on to quote

Romans 6:23: "The wages of sin is death. . . ." That
means the consequence of being imperfect is death. That
wasn't what I wanted to hear! The best news mankind could
hear was in the second part of the verse: **". . . but the gift
of God is eternal life through Jesus Christ." Ephesians
2: 8 & 9** says, **"For by grace are you saved through
faith; and not of yourselves, it is a gift of God . . . not of
works, lest any should boast."**

Brother James explained that salvation was not
something we could get by being good. We could never earn
it or buy it . . . only by accepting it as a gift.

For the first time I understood that God's love and
forgiveness wasn't based on my goodness or what I could do;
it was based on Christ's perfection and what He had done on
the cross for me.

So I did what anyone must do to accept that gift; I
gave all that I knew about me to all that I knew about Jesus.
And He accepted me just as I am!

Many people know all the facts about Jesus and yet
He isn't real to them. They don't know Him personally. It is

like knowing all about the President of the United States but not knowing him personally. When someone gives you a gift, it is not truly yours until you accept it.

This was the most important decision I ever made. It would change my perspective on things that would happen to me later in life, and . . . it would give me strength to go on.

Since that time, there have been many frightening experiences and challenges. The first day of junior high school was scary . . . so much peer pressure, even then. I wanted to look just right, not too different, yet I wanted some attention. I recollect that being a lowly freshman in high school brought great anxiety. Though I do not recall what I wore on each of those days, I do remember exactly how I felt. Like the scared little girl in the green and white dress, I wondered how I would handle this new challenge. Going away to Oklahoma State University was traumatic. Leaving a small town, where everyone knew me and I knew everyone, was a giant step into the unknown.

It was at Oklahoma State University that I met my prince charming. David Miller came charging into my life, not on a white horse but in a dependable white Ford. We had so much in common! Both our mothers were teachers and our fathers were Oklahoma wheat farmers. We soon began to plan our lives, wanting to marry and to have children together.

On a hot August Saturday evening, I walked down the aisle of my little church in Pond Creek, Oklahoma, and became Mrs. David Miller. I'm sure that I looked like most brides of the day wearing a traditional white empire-waist gown. I straightened my shoulders and stood very tall and confident, but on the inside I again felt like that little school girl. More than anything I wanted to be the best wife, cook, homemaker, lover, and ultimately . . . mother.

Not long after the honeymoon, I discovered that all those paperback romance novels that I had devoured as a teenager did not adequately prepare me for marriage. I found that I had married a man who had a mind of his own and was as stubborn as I! If I tried tactfully to suggest that we should do something, he would reply, "My family never did it that way." It would take the wind right out of my sails, and I realized that this thing called marriage was much more complex than I had thought.

Three years after we married, while David was in medical school at Oklahoma University, we began the biggest challenge yet . . . parenthood. Manda Lynn came bouncing into the world on December 9, 1968.

Being an avid reader, I studied every baby book on the shelves, but I couldn't find her "type" in any of those volumes. This baby did not like to eat or sleep on any set schedule. She didn't care for her crib, her infant seat or her swing; she simply preferred to be held upright in her mother's arms at all times. Consequently, I learned to hold her on my left hip while I cooked, ironed, and cleaned with my right hand. Most mothers know exactly what I am talking about, especially if they have more than one child.

In spite of my being a very amateur mother, Manda grew up into a fine young woman who finished college and married a wonderful man named Todd Vermillion. She now has a growing memory box of her own and has also learned that the institution of marriage is more complex than she thought.

Three years later, September 10, 1971, in Irving, Texas, Jennifer Alaine was born. No two sisters have been so different. I'm sure that if we had been blessed with a dozen children, each would have presented his or her own unique challenges!

Jenny graduated from Baylor University in May 1993. She is presently a graduate student at the University of Missouri in Kansas City.

Both Manda and Jenny have grown into women of whom I am very proud.

In 1974 I was again "with child." Pregnant women can have some weird thoughts. I remember thinking that it would be nice to have a boy for my husband. I loved my girls so much, and it would be fun to have another that I could dress in pretty dresses with ribbons and lace. I secretly wondered if I could love a boy as much as I loved the girls.

Pat Breckenridge

Jason Scott Miller exploded into the world on December 28, 1974, weighing 9 pounds and 9 ounces! He was born in Jacksonville, Florida, while David was serving in the Navy. I looked into his beautiful brown eyes and fell in love. How ridiculous I had been to entertain the thought that I might not love him as much as I loved the girls. Jason was all boy! From the time he could make sounds, he mimicked trucks and planes, and from very early, he loved sports of all kinds.

With three children under 7 years old, we moved to Springfield, Missouri, for David to begin his practice.

We found a church, school, Mother's Day Out program and became involved in our community. We began to pay off debts that we had accrued in college and in medical school. Things were going according to the American dream for the first couple of years, but I soon realized that our marriage was in trouble.

No matter how hard I tried, we just couldn't seem to get along. We went to three marriage counselors . . . without success. One day David called me and said, "Pat, I don't love you anymore and I want a divorce."

Never had I felt such rejection. I had such a sense of failure and felt afraid and vulnerable. I had always thought it would work out; now after 15 long years of marriage and three children, my husband was going to leave me. It was so unfair. I'd given the marriage everything I could. Perhaps I had expected too much; perhaps I was too idealistic or had too much pride. I don't know; nor do I know what I could have done differently.

There were tough times, especially with three children ages 5, 8, and 11. Bedtime often took as long as two hours, with many tears and so many questions to be answered.

I remember one night especially when Jason looked at me and asked, "Mommy, who will teach me how to be a man?" I gulped, said a quick prayer and replied, "Jason, you just be a good boy every day and you'll grow up to be a fine man."

After those emotionally draining bedtimes, I would stand in my shower and cry out to God for strength. In **Hebrews 13:5**, Jesus said, **"I will never leave you or forsake you."** What a promise! The Lord is so wonderful-- He is never too busy, never tells my secrets, and never breaks a promise. I have learned that everyone else may leave or fail, but He never will!

I decided that my main objective was to be the best mother that I could be. The children would climb onto my bed each night, and we would read the Psalms or Proverbs and discuss them. I asked God to protect my children. My prayer was that they would never be scarred by the divorce or allow it to be an excuse for not reaching their full potential.

I had no plans to remarry. The statistics are not great for second marriages, and learning to live with someone at middle age sounded like a very difficult thing. Having to adjust to his idiosyncrasies along with the blending of families didn't sound easy. I was sure that must be why second marriages had a greater failure rate than first marriages.

Out of the blue about a year later, the phone rang and an old familiar voice said, "Is this the girl who wore the yellow skirt and sweater on our first date in high school?" How impressed I was that a man could remember what I had worn almost 20 years ago!

Dennis had been my first love. We had dated during most of my high school years. He was one of those memories that I had wrapped in pink tissue paper and carefully tucked in my memory box.

As we talked, we discussed mutual friends, family, and our lives. It was fun to "catch up" on all that had happened in the eighteen years since we had last seen each other. He said he was going to Branson for a business-pleasure trip and suggested that we might get together. I told him that I was glad to hear from him and wished him well but that I felt it was not the right time to see each other. He agreed and we said goodbye. I knew that I had said the right thing, but I am a woman, and I would have loved to see this "memory" again.

The months passed. Finally, on my birthday in October, I received a card. I immediately recognized the handwriting and tore open the envelope. All it said was, "Happy Birthday, Dennis." That was "all" it said. I looked on the back and on the inside. I even shook it but nothing else was there. Again, I was impressed that he would remember my birthday after all those years.

The following January, Dennis phoned. By this time I had given considerable thought to the situation, and I believe God had prepared me for the next step. Dennis asked if I felt it was the right time. I responded "YES," wanting to add, "GET OVER HERE!"

We exchanged letters along with photographs. I was delighted to see that Dennis still had plenty of hair and all his teeth. He looked very much like the boy I had a high school crush on, except now he was a man. He must have liked what he saw in my picture because he made plans to come to Springfield when he was in Branson in February.

It is ridiculous how a grown woman with three small children feels when she is about to see her high school sweetheart. I didn't know what to say, how I would welcome him, or what to do with the children. So I took my mother's suggestion to bring them over to her house for the evening.

Dennis took me out to dinner and to a movie. It was amazing how quickly the years melted away and how comfortable we felt with each other. What is most important, I discovered that he loved the Lord as much as I did!

Over the next few months we talked and prayed about our future. Before long, we felt it was right and good for us to be joined as husband and wife. On June 17, 1982, I became Mrs. Dennis Breckenridge.

Second marriages are hard, extremely hard. We tried to blend our resources and personalities, along with my three children and his son Brad, who lived with us part of the time. During many of those years, we had three teenagers under our roof. That meant alternately staying up on our toes and down on our knees.

A couple of our children got into things they shouldn't have. We had to practice tough love, and THAT'S TOUGH! Like any other parents of our generation, we found with startling realization that our kids faced a much different world than we had faced as teenagers. Peer pressure is much greater and with so many more options. Two of our children had a real struggle with self-esteem, which was displayed in a variety of ways. One child was very vocal and openly rebellious; the other was very quiet. Both got into trouble with alcohol.

We made visits to the jail and took part in drug rehabilitation and family counseling. We set some firm guidelines and prayed for ourselves and for our children. During that time, God showed me how I look in His holy eyes, sometimes rebelling quietly and sometimes verbally. I saw myself doing my own thing and expressing doubt about His divine wisdom and His claim on my life. Like my own children, I have often run away from God, only to fall down, skin my knees, and bloody my nose.

But God was faithful! I have always loved those two little words, "BUT GOD." Throughout the scripture we see impending disaster for an individual or even for a race of people. Then we read the words, "BUT GOD." I am reminded that as our Heavenly Father, He always holds onto us, watches over us, and protects us. He will always give us a hand up when we are down.

During the worst part of one of my children's rebellions, I asked God to take my own life if it would help my child. I truly did tell the Lord that I would give up my life physically if it would help to have me out of the picture. I was totally serious; you don't offer your life to God lightly. He obviously did not take me up on my offer. I do believe that prayer opened the door for God to work in my life and in the life of my child. To offer one's life on the altar means different things to different people. For me, it meant that I completely let go of the situation, knowing I was absolutely helpless.

It has, therefore, been music to this mother's ears to hear some of the lessons my children have learned. It is truly amazing what they grasp and remember. One of my daughters gave me a great compliment. She said I was the wisest person she knew. If only she realized how lacking in wisdom I felt during her "growing-up" years. Another daughter told me she was glad I had taught her that she could get through whatever she had to do. This was during her freshman year in college when some of the kids were quitting. If only she knew how many times I had felt I couldn't go on another day. Sometimes, both daughters have been critical. They have told me I was inflexible, but I reminded them that they always knew where I stood and where the boundaries were.

Being a parent has been the most rewarding but the most difficult job I have ever done. The responsibility to teach and to train a child is surely overwhelming. Many parents are weighed down by guilt because they feel they have failed. If we commit ourselves to God and to raising our children according to His precepts, I believe He will bless us and our children. That doesn't mean the rough times won't come or that our children will always do what we would like them to do.

Once when I was feeling like an inadequate mother, God reminded me of His first two kids, Adam and Eve. He put them in a perfect world and surrounded them with good food and beauty. They had everything they needed. He wasn't too strict with them, giving them only one rule. He was firm in that they would suffer the consequences if they disobeyed and ate fruit of the tree of knowledge. Even in a perfect setting, without TV or crime, and having a perfect Heavenly Father, Adam and Eve still made the choice to sin. We have all been given the freedom by God Himself to choose our actions and reactions. With this in mind, is it any wonder that our children rebel? We must not blame ourselves for our children's choices or our own parents for our decisions.

Not only did we have children to raise through difficult times, but we also suffered through job changes and financial reverses. I knew what it was like "to have it" and "not to have it"; but the Lord sustained us.

Dennis was an insurance salesman, which meant he worked on commission only. My father was a wheat farmer and I knew that farmers lived by faith. I learned that men on commission also must live by faith.

Four years into our marriage, Dennis was found to have melanoma on his back. The doctor removed it and said that he believed it was in an early stage and would probably not recur. Fifteen months later, it had metastasized through his lymph system to a large node under his arm. He had 20 lymph nodes removed. This time the doctor was not optimistic. He told us that the cancer would probably recur within a year. It could be in his lungs, brain, liver, or all over his body.

That evening I slipped down to my knees by my bed and prayed, "Father, you know that I like being married. I don't like being single very much, so I"m asking you to heal my husband . . . please give us more time together."

We talked to physicians all over the country. They concurred that the prognosis wasn't good. Radiation and chemotherapy have proven to be effective, but not a cure.

We investigated several research programs and decided to be a part of one at the University of Arkansas.

Sometimes I think it is good that God doesn't let us see too far down the road of life. I did not realize how much I would need my husband to support and be with me in the years ahead.

Every year my son Jason traveled with his dad (my first husband) to the annual Oklahoma University vs. Nebraska football game. On November 19, 1988, Jason and his dad traveled to Oklahoma for the game. Usually Jason took a friend along, but there were no extra tickets that year, so Jason and his dad took off alone in David's single-engine Bonanza airplane.

Being from Oklahoma, all in our family are avid OU fans, so Dennis and I watched the game on television. It was a miserable day for football, the weather was cold and wet, and to make it worse . . . we lost.

After the game, I prepared dinner for friends we had invited that evening. They came, ate and left. As I cleaned the kitchen, I began to feel a little apprehension in the pit of my stomach. My ears strained to hear a car drive up, the front door open, or the phone ring. But a car didn't drive up, the door didn't open, and the phone didn't ring.

My insides felt more and more like jelly as the hour grew late. Again, I felt like the frightened little girl in the green and white dress.

At 12:40 A.M. two men came to my door. I remember hearing the car doors and watching them come up the front walk. They told us the plane had run into trouble immediately upon departure. The wings had iced and the gyroscope had failed. David had declared an emergency landing in Oklahoma City, but as he tried to land, the plane stalled, crashed, and exploded.

Nothing in life can prepare you for the pain of losing a child. Even the idea of it was so painful that my mind would run away from it. And yet, I had to deal with the realization that my only son was gone from this earth. I would never again feel his bony arms hugging me. I would never smell that "boy" smell after he played outdoors. I would not experience the joy of seeing him grow into an adult -- to become a father, which he had told me he could hardly wait to be! He loved children and they loved him. How could this happen? I had always prayed for protection over my children. Hadn't He heard me?

Shortly after Jason's death, I felt numb and yet strangely very aware. I could see parts of Jason's body in close detail. It was as though my mind were taking photographs so that I could always remember him and how he looked. I saw the scar on his knee, his eyebrows, the way his hair grew on his neck, the pores of his skin. I remembered his facial and body expressions and the sound of his voice. Jenny, my younger daughter, panicked because she couldn't remember such details.

My heart went out to Jenny and Manda. At ages 18 and 20, they had lost a parent and a brother, while I still had both my parents. Life seemed out of order. I hurt for them as I saw them struggling with this new experience of death. They asked me who would give them away at their weddings, what we would do about the holidays, and how they were supposed to feel or act.

Pat Breckenridge

We all agreed later that it was as if we were watching someone else go through the motions. We felt detached and unemotional at times, confused and lost at others.

I remember hearing stories on the news of someone's losing a family member, and I would think, "How awful for them." Then with a sharp pain, I realized this is exactly what had happened to us. One day I was ironing when a news bulletin came over the TV about the plane crash over Lockerbie, England. I shrank to my knees as my whole being empathized with the families that had loved ones on that flight.

I had read that if our loved ones are with the Lord and He is in us, then they can't be far away. This took on real meaning for me. Truly, I did feel Jason was very close. Although I could not see or touch him, he seemed just beyond my fingertips. Heaven seemed very near. I had heard others say that Heaven becomes much sweeter and more a reality when a loved one dies. That proved true for me, also. My feet seemed much less rooted to this earth.

My daughter Jenny had a very difficult time leaving for college in Texas that next fall. She worried about my having an "empty nest." She felt as if she were abandoning me. I assured her that I would be fine and that she must go on with her life through the door God had opened for her. With a rather mature perspective, she said, "Well, Mom, I guess it isn't such a big deal to send a kid off to college in another state when you already have one in Heaven." I agreed, but in my heart I knew that I would worry more about her. That was one of the benefits I had discovered after Jason had left this earth. I no longer stewed and fretted about Jason's doing his lessons, making the soccer team, or being happy. God had given me the sweet assurance that Jason was just fine--never better!

Words are so inadequate to describe the way God ministered to me and through me. I missed Jason, and my grief overwhelmed me at times. When allowing myself to think about those last few moments before the plane crashed and the fear Jason might have felt, I would feel weak. I would call out to God for help, and He would always

whisper to me, "Jason is fine. I've got him. He's home."
Peace would flow through me immediately. I know that
Jason is home and I will one day be there, too!

During the three days following the crash,
approximately 200 people came to our house. I stood in the
entry way to greet them because I felt each person was sent
from God. They were God's arms around me, comforting
me. In turn, I felt Him in me, comforting others. Most of
the people didn't know what to say, but I did not need their
words as much as I needed their touch. Some of them were
people I hardly knew, yet they seemed like old friends.
Because they had been a part of our loved one's life, they
were now able to share our grief.

In the weeks and months to follow, people sent
letters, pictures, videos and remembrances of Jason. Every
one of those was a treasure to me. It was especially helpful
when people talked to me about him. Many people thought
it would be painful for them to mention Jason, so they said
nothing. I understood because I had probably done the same
thing myself. But I had Jason on my mind and in my heart

constantly, and it was such a joy to know that other people were thinking of him, too.

Many permanent memorials were also given. Among these gifts were more than 100 Gideon Bibles, trees planted, soccer field memorials, donations given in his name for library books, children's organizations, and others. Each was a love gift to our family.

Sometimes I would imagine Jason, with his impish grin, smiling down on all the activities and people. He loved people; he loved celebrations; and most of all, he loved Jesus.

People have said to me, "What a sad thing that Jason's life was cut so short." I believe that Jason had a complete and very full life. He had great influence on his peers because of the life he lived and because of his death. Over 200 junior high students attended his funeral. Many brought flowers to the grave afterwards. Parents told me how Jason's death affected their children. One mother wrote that of all of her daughter's friends, she had liked Jason the best. He was bright and had a wonderful sense of humor.

Most of all, she said, he was so kind and always an encourager to others.

One of Jason's best friends wrote that when Jason was around, her troubles disappeared. She said, "Jason was the sweetest person I've ever known. He never did anything to hurt anyone. Never did I hear him talk behind someone's back. Jason always made me feel like I fit in even if I didn't."

Another wrote, "Jason was one of the neatest people I've ever known. He never acted less than a Christian at school, and he always stood strong. He influenced so many of his friends and was such a good witness. You couldn't help being happy around him. I have no doubt that Jason is with the Lord."

Monday, after the crash, a tribute to Jason was read over the intercom at Jason's school. Luis Rey, the student body president and a good friend, read: "Jason Miller passed away Saturday night in a plane accident along with his father. Many of us knew Jason and we will miss him greatly. I know Jason would want us to know that he is in a much better place now--because of his faith, trust and commitment to Jesus Christ. Now we can truly see that life is like a vapor. We have only today; we are not promised tomorrow. We love you, Jason . . . ." A recording of "Friends Are Friends Forever" was then played.

Jason has gone to a better place, and we who knew him are left with a heart full of memories.

Within a very short time after Jason's death, God filled me to overflowing with gratitude that I had been given Jason. What a gift he had been--a gift I never deserved. Jason had been taken away from me, but he had been with me for almost 14 years. He taught me much about life and living it to the fullest. Jason loved life; he loved people; and most of all, he loved Jesus.

Not long before he died, we were having a mother and son talk. I asked him how he was doing at school with the other kids. (He was in the eighth grade and peer pressure was a real thing!) Jason looked at me with those very big brown eyes and said, "Well, Mother, I guess I'm sort of a popular wimp." Amused, I asked him to explain. Since he didn't smoke, drink or chew, some of his friends made fun of him. I asked him how that made him feel. He thought about it for a minute and replied, "I feel O.K." I told him all that mattered was his relationship to God and how he felt about himself. He said, "I know that, Mom."

Jason was not perfect. He was a procrastinator and sometimes demanding, but he was the best son that I could have had. I miss him and know that I always will, but I know where he is. He's home, and one day I'll be there, too!

People have asked me how I have handled his death as well as I have. I can give only one reason: I know that God has my son Jason in Heaven with Him, just as I have His son Jesus here in my heart.

One of my favorite things is a snowflake. After an Ozark snowfall, I often find myself drawn to the window sill where the sun is streaming in and the snowflakes are stuck to the glass. It will always be a wonder to me that we have such a creative Heavenly Father, who can make each snowflake into a uniquely intricate, delicate pattern. In the center of each snowflake must be a dust particle on which the pattern is begun. We are like that. God made each of us uniquely different. Sometimes we have circumstances that come into our lives that are painful, seemingly unnecessary, and even dirty. Our magnificent God can take those unwanted events and make beautiful designs out of our lives.

It has been seven years since Dennis has dealt with cancer, and he has had no recurrence. Melanoma isn't considered cured for ten years. We have met people who have gone eight or nine years without recurrence. Knowing this has helped us to be thankful for every day and to keep our priorities straight.

My children are grown now and eternity will not be long enough to praise God for His protection, His wisdom, His mercy and grace! Last April 25, 1995, God gave us little Jeremy David Vermillion.

I believe everything that happens to us makes us who we are. If we were to subtract even one experience, we would not be all that God intended for us to be. Bad things happen to believers so that others can see the difference that Jesus makes in the difficult times. I cannot say I am glad that I divorced, that my husband has cancer, or that my son died. I can, however, praise God for loving me enough to prove His great sufficiency through it all!

Pat Breckenridge, mother of three, is a regional representative for Stonecroft Ministries, (Christian Women's Clubs) and a popular speaker. She and her husband Dennis live in Springfield, MO.

Lori Trice

I was born in 1959 in Lawton, Oklahoma. My mother was sixteen and unmarried when she found herself pregnant with me. Had abortion been as convenient then as it is now, I am convinced I would not be here today. She and my 20-year-old dad decided to be married.

When I was 3 years old, my family, which now included my 2-year-old sister, moved into a new subdivision. Our new house was one that Dad helped design and build. My daddy made sure the builders carefully followed every detail. My grandma tells me he would measure each room to ensure that everything was perfect. Dad was always taking pictures, so I have lots to look at and remember. The three-bedroom, two-bath house was red brick with a white front door and white shutters. Mom and Dad enjoyed working in the yard planting flowers and shrubs. We had a beautifully landscaped yard with the best barefoot grass in the neighborhood. All the neighborhood kids came to our house to play.

Mom made curtains to match the canopy beds in the room that my sister and I shared. My dad built bookshelves for our room and the den. I can still remember sitting in the two-car garage, hearing the sound of the table saw and smelling the freshly cut wood. I have many happy childhood memories.

My parents had many friends. They had lived in Lawton most of their lives and were always willing to lend a helping hand to their friends. They would do anything from hanging wallpaper to installing a fence. Dad had worked for the local newspaper since high school. Mom worked for the local utility company and attended school at night. She sought a teaching degree so she could spend the summers with my sister and me.

Our house and family were "picture perfect," on the outside. Inside, I saw a completely different picture. I was often awakened to arguing, crying, and hurtful words. I didn't always witness the fights, but the next morning I would find broken glass, not quite swept up, and a cut on

Lori Trice

Mom's eye that would tell me what had happened the night before.

Because of my father's physical abuse of her, my mom would often pack suitcases and the three of us would go nearby to her parents' home. I was always glad to leave the instability of our home and go to live with my grandma and grandpa. They didn't go to church, but it was plain to see how much they loved each other and that gave me a sense of security. I was always disappointed when Mom said it was time to go home.

When my sister and I were 8 and 9 years old, we moved to the country where my parents planned to remodel an older home. The house sat on ten acres, and I enjoyed climbing trees and taking long walks across the open fields. Gazing at the beautiful twinkling stars at night and embracing the beauty that surrounded me, I became acquainted with God, the Creator.

Shortly after the move to the country, my father lost his job. I was a little older now and began to see the pressure on my dad. Both Mom and Dad were drinking almost daily, and I watched as alcohol brought destruction to our already unstable home.

My father was a perfectionist in the things he did and the way he wanted things to be. His garage was perfectly neat and well organized. His perfect life, however, was breaking apart--beyond his control.

That summer, a college friend of my mom's agreed to let her teenage daughter baby-sit my sister and me along with her own younger brother and sister. The last thing this teenage girl wanted to do all summer was to baby-sit four kids under 12. So when a local church offered Vacation Bible School, she sent every one of us.

Something special happened to me in that little church. When the preacher spoke, it seemed as if he were speaking only to me in that crowded room. He said that Jesus loved even me, and that He died to pay for my sins. I understood that I was a sinner and my sin had separated me from a God who loved me. I knew that I needed something better in my life. When I recognized my need for a Savior, God showed me Jesus. I talked to God right then, and, as a little girl at the age of 8 or 9, gave my life to the Lord Jesus. I didn't understand the impact that decision would have on the rest of my life.

I can write to you today because of that choice so many years ago. Being introduced to the Lord Jesus Christ and growing in a relationship with Him has brought me through things too difficult for me to have handled alone.

Many of you have had kids in vacation bible school who where there simply because you were a free baby-sitter. I was one of those kids. From now on, look differently at the faces of those young lives who visit your church. You may never know how God will use you as His instrument to change a child's life.

When I was 12 years old, my mother told my sister and me that she and Dad were divorcing and we would be moving in with my grandparents. I was relieved that finally our unhappy home life was ending. I wanted a family like those on television, where the children shouted for joy when Daddy came home. I had tried and tried to do everything I could to make it happen, but it was too big a job for me. I was sure the divorce would solve all of my unhappy family problems. Later I would realize that divorce usually makes things worse instead of better.

One day after we had moved to my grandparents' home, my dad called Mom and told her he had set fire to our house in the country. He had threatened this before so Mom feared it might be true.

Mom and I picked up my sister from sixth-grade cheerleading practice and picked up a friend of Mom's who had been helping her through the divorce. When we arrived at the house, we found it engulfed in flames. We drove to a neighbor's house and called the fire department. As we were returning to the house, we met my daddy. He had what looked like a shotgun sticking out of the driver's side window. He ran us off the road, and the car came to an abrupt stop just as a shotgun blast shattered both side windows and instantly killed my mother's friend. My sister jumped out of the back seat and crouched on the ground for safety between the car and the ditch. Just then, Dad pulled over and leaned inside the car to see my Mom slumped over, apparently unconscious. I cried to him, "Daddy, what are you doing? Why are you doing this?" Then he said to me, but more to himself, "I have to do this; I have to." He reached inside his car and pulled out a gun. Then he put the gun under my mom's chin and with one shot--killed her!

Many emotions flood my heart as I recall the events of that day, October 6, 1971. As I remember Daddy, I hurt for him because of the hurt and despair he must have felt. I think of my mom and the anguish that she must have lived with every day. Although Mother was beautiful, I don't remember her smiling very much.

While sitting in that back seat and talking to my daddy, I had no fear for my own life. I knew that he loved me. Furthermore, I realized that in the midst of their extreme hurt, both my parents loved my sister and me very much.

In one quick instant, as Daddy looked at the devastation before him, he seemed to come to the reality of what he had done. He said, "Oh my God!" As if in a daze, he put the gun to his own head and with one shot, he fell to the ground--dead!

I stepped out of the car, over my daddy's body, and ran frantically down the road toward the fire truck.

The next thing I remember is sitting in a police car with my arms around my 11-year-old sister and telling her I loved her. I asked the police officer to call my grandma and gave them the phone number. I knew Grandma would come to get us and make everything better, like she always did.

Suddenly, I heard the police radio dispatcher. "The grandmother has been shot." Before we had met Daddy on the road, he had gone to town and tried to kill my grandma. She later told me that Daddy fired the gun several times at her. She lay on the floor pretending to be dead and hoping he would leave her alone. Finally, he did.

My grandma spent several weeks in intensive care. She was shot several times in her head and chest, and she lost sight in one eye. After a miraculous recovery, she and grandpa, at 46 and 51 years of age, took on the tremendous responsibility of parenting two girls, 11 and 12 years old.

Lori Trice

I wish I could tell you the years with my grandparents were easy. We all had pain to deal with: my sister and I with the brutal deaths of our parents, our grandparents with the brutal death of their daughter and son-in-law, and the long, painful physical rehabilitation of my grandmother. These problems were added to the normal trials of just being a family.

Totally immersing myself in school was my attempt to find comfort. High school friends, school club activities, and especially music became my life. I was excited about the future, and more than anything I wanted to go to college.

I received a scholarship in music to Cameron University in Lawton, Oklahoma. The new-found freedom of college life was exhilarating. Everything revolved around my friends and our college music department. My time was my own, and I could spend it on whatever I wanted. Unfortunately, college academics were not a priority with me; there were too many new boys to know.

By the end of my freshman year, I was certain I had met my future husband. I looked forward to building a family like the one I had always wanted, a family centered on love and commitment and church. Everyone thought we were the perfect couple. I was ready to get married; however, he was beginning his junior year and was serious about his education.

Our relationship continued, and one day, at 18 years old, I found that I was pregnant. I then realized I didn't want to be married and certainly didn't want a child. I was terrified of what people would think of me if they knew our relationship had gone this far. I knew that sex before marriage was wrong. I didn't plan to have a sexual relationship. I just didn't plan, at all! Things just happened. Now I was forced to plan.

Planned Parenthood had previously come to my high school, so I went to them for help. They counseled me about having an abortion. To erase this "mistake" seemed like a good idea. My boyfriend had transferred to a college in another state; we scheduled the abortion to be done there. No one would ever need to know.

Having made this mistake, I needed a new start. My best high school friend attended the University of North Texas where she had received a music scholarship. This was the best music school in our part of the country. I was accepted as a transfer student. My audition for the music department was a humbling experience. I was one talent among hundreds of other talented musicians, and my auditions didn't qualify me for anything special. Devastated, I changed my major to Psychology.

The disco era was in full swing, so my social calendar filled quickly with dates and dancing. Dancing can be innocent enough; but where there was dancing, there was also alcohol, sometimes free drinks. After a year at this "big city college," I was in over my head with dates, drinking, and disco.

My stay at this school was short lived. Grandma didn't like the changes she was seeing in me and wanted me a little closer to home. She talked me into transferring to a Christian university where she had already made an appointment for me to speak with the admission's counselor.

The school was small, but the campus was beautiful; and I wanted the safety and security that seemed to pervade this Christian campus (I'm quite sure my grandma wanted the same). Although my grades were poor, I was admitted on probation. Optimistically, I looked forward to this chance for a new beginning.

Our God is a God of new beginnings. **Lamentations 3:22** says, **"It is of the Lord's mercies that we are not consumed, because His compassions fail not. They are new every morning; great is Thy faithfulness."** In **Proverbs 3:5-6,** the Bible says, **"Trust in the Lord with all your heart and do not rely on your own insight. In all your ways acknowledge Him and He will direct your paths."** I knew that my past choices had not honored God; they were not God's best for me. I dedicated myself, at this new beginning, to follow Him and seek His direction for my life. I put my trust in God and became active in church. I studied the Bible and attended discipleship Bible studies on campus. I asked God to find a husband for me since I had no luck finding him myself. I prayed for my future mate as I had never prayed before.

After my first year at the Christian college, I met my future husband. I had been looking for him for a long time (it seemed like an eternity). The campus sponsored a "Dating Game," and I was asked to be a bachelorette who would choose a date from three bachelors. When it was time to make my decision, I chose Brent Trice, who swept me off my feet (I had met him earlier and recognized his voice).

The first time I saw him, I was breathless. He was tall, with strong shoulders. His clear blue eyes seemed to look straight into my heart. When I asked friends about Brent, I discovered that he was called to preach and was considering foreign mission work. Brent had given his life to Jesus Christ at 16 years of age and was serving as a youth minister at a local church. I also felt that God was leading me into Christian service. I loved Jesus with all my heart and wanted to accomplish big things for Him. Serving in the ministry was the biggest thing I could think of doing for my

Lord. As Brent and I grew closer in our relationship, we made plans to serve Him together in the ministry.

Eight months after we met, we were married. We committed ourselves and our marriage to the Lord. **"Delight yourself also in the Lord; and He shall give thee the desires of thine heart. Commit thy way unto the Lord; trust also in Him; and He shall bring it to pass." Psalm 37:3-4.** I was living out the dream of a lifetime -- a happy marriage and future family.

A week after the wedding, we joined our first church in our new hometown of Oklahoma City. We attended seminars and read all the books we could find on marriage. In our first few years together, we focused on our responsibilities: jobs at local banks and Brent's working on his bachelor's degree. The private Christian university was too expensive for us to afford. Therefore, Brent transferred to the University of Central Oklahoma, in Edmond, a suburb of Oklahoma City.

After three years, our first child, Katie Marie, was born. We were so excited to be parents. I quit my job to be home with Kati; and just 16 months later, we had our second child, Kennedy Brent.

Brent finally graduated and now believed that he could better serve God in the business world. He went to work with his father in the mid 1980's and quickly climbed the ladder of success.

We lived in a large house in an affluent part of Oklahoma City. A swimming pool and hot tub were in the backyard of this four-bedroom, three-bath home. I loved my kitchen with its Jennair stove and dishwasher, an ice machine, a trash compactor, and a double-door refrigerator with ice and water in the door. We had every necessity--and more!

A housekeeper came every couple of weeks. I put my dry cleaning and dirty laundry on the front porch and the following day would find clean, starched clothes. We belonged to the country club where my husband's family had a corporate membership. Our children went to private school. Several times a year, we vacationed in Florida and Hawaii. Our family had a yacht and boats at the lake; the kids loved to go there to spend the weekend. We would take the company plane for shopping or visiting friends.

We drove fine cars. My husband's company car was a Lincoln Towncar, and I drove the all-American mother's taxi, a minivan. Each, of course, was equipped with its own phone. Speaking of cars, Grandmommie (Brent's mother) would take the children through McDonald's drive-through in her Rolls Royce. They loved to eat their lunch on the little pull down trays in the back seat.

When I was expecting our third child, Kristi Leigh, I purchased new furniture with pink satin and lacy frills for her canopy bed. Life was good by anybody's standards; but to be honest, we wanted more. Our house wasn't in the "best" neighborhood. We wanted each child to have his or her "own" bathroom, and we really wanted another living area--more, more, more!

Brent and I had always realized the importance of God's Word and had given it priority in our lives. We taught a Bible study class for young marrieds in our church. We knew the importance of a church family. The Bible said "**not to forsake the assembly together.**" During those prosperous, affluent years, we felt privileged to give to the church and to people in need.

Brent had what I believed to be the perfect job. The salary was comfortable. It was perfect because he worked for his family. We had <u>security!</u> I didn't worry that one day he would come home and say that he'd been fired or laid off (as had happened to so many of our friends).

I felt certain of the future. In her book "Pain is Inevitable but Misery is Optional so Stick a Geranium in Your Hat and be Happy," Barbara Johnson says, "My future is so bright, I need sunglasses!" That described my feeling of security.

Brent traveled occasionally but was never away for more than a few days. I didn't mind his short trips because I could always go SHOPPING. I loved to SHOP!

I began to see that although this job was perfect for me, it was not perfect for my husband. Because of the conflicts between Brent and his father, there were conflicts between Brent and his Heavenly Father. The dissension involved issues of integrity that were of growing concern to Brent. He had mentioned quitting several times but never had my approval because I just wasn't ready to give up all of those "things" that made my life so comfortable.

And my life was comfortable, happy and predictable until the phone call on that sunny afternoon. I had just come home from leading a Precept Bible Study on the book of **l Peter**. The theme of **l Peter** is persevering in trials and suffering. In **I Peter 1:6** the scripture says, **"In this you greatly rejoice, even though now for a little while, IF NECESSARY, you have been distressed by various trials,"** then God Himself explains why; **"that the proof of your faith being more precious than gold which is perishable even though tested by fire may be found to result in praise and glory and honor at the revelation of the Lord Jesus Christ."**

I had no idea the direction my life was about to take as I picked up the phone. Brent called to say that he just couldn't do it anymore. He had quit his job.

Lori Trice

We entered the ranks of the unemployed--not a comfortable position to be in, by any means. But I knew, there were people at our church who had persevered through the trial of unemployment, and I knew that they would pray us through it. **Psalm 55** says, **"they are many that strive with me."** I knew--just as Aaron and Hur held up Moses' arms--that my friends would pray for me and help me through it. And they did.

For years I had read through the book of **Proverbs**. There are 31 chapters in **Proverbs** and 31 days in a month, a proverb for every day. I would read God's words in **Proverbs 21: "Do not weary yourself to gain wealth, cease from your consideration of it, when you set your eyes on it, it is gone. For certainly wealth makes itself wings, like an eagle that flies toward the heavens."** I knew I was not to set my eyes on wealth, because I knew that it could be gone as quick as a wink. You never really believe it will happen to you, especially when you work for your family.

I began to pray for my husband in a different way. I prayed that God would lead him to the job that He had for him. I was convinced that God wanted Brent to work and I also knew that He had a job perfectly suited for the talents He had given him. I prayed diligently and daily. I couldn't forget because our daily life was a constant reminder to pray. It was my responsibility as a wife to lift him up before the Father.

I thought the **"distressed by various trials, for a little while"** meant probably that by the end of the summer he would have another job. As I prayed, in the back of my mind, I knew the job would be just like the one he had before. His new job would enable us to enjoy that kind of lifestyle again. But that wasn't God's plan.

One detail of the "before picture" that I left out is that we had just moved into a bigger house, one with a mortgage payment. We made many mistakes and wrong choices during that time. We were shown and I want you to know that God is sufficient even when we fail miserably.

Our money was low, so we started to sell some "stuff." We participated in a neighborhood garage sale and put out all the excess . . . and did we ever have plenty! We made several hundred dollars. I thought, "This is great; this is all we need to help us through." Certainly by the time this money ran out, Brent would have a good job. Well, the money came and went, as money does, and he still didn't have a job. We had a big house and fine cars, but we didn't have the money we needed to live.

During those affluent days, the money was there to buy things like fur coats and jewelry. As you could probably guess, a mink coat doesn't sell very quickly during a hot, Oklahoma summer. I love jewelry. On our eighth anniversary I received a two-carat diamond solitaire (of course, I picked it out). My wedding ring was the most valuable item we could sell, and since we had sold most of our furniture, I was glad that I could sell it. I think it was easier for me to sell it since I had initiated the purchase and had picked it out myself. Again, I was certain that by the time this money was spent, all our troubles would be over and Brent would have his "perfect" job.

As I kept selling things and getting deeper into this trial, my enthusiasm and optimism ran out. I began to face reality. This wasn't going to be over quickly. My self-esteem hit a new low. If any one of your husbands has ever been unemployed, you know that the self-esteem goes quickly. I was praying for Brent, but I was not feeling good about myself. I just wanted to stay in my house, close the curtains, and not answer the door.

But I knew my Lord, and I knew that He is sufficient. I had stood before Bible study groups and Sunday school classes and talked about the sufficiency of Christ. Now, just like I Peter had said, He was testing my faith, to prove me. My relationship with the Lord Jesus drew me out of my hurt and caused me to come and "assemble together" with the people of God "in the sanctuary of the Lord." And when I came, my church family surrounded me with the loving arms of Jesus. Even though in our minds we know our Lord is with us in tough times, we

Lori Trice

need to experience the love (a touch, a hug) of other humans to assure us of His presence.

In **Deuteronomy 8,** the Bible speaks of the children of Israel (and of me) while in the wilderness: **"And He humbled you and let you be hungry and fed you with manna which you did not know."** When my freezer was totally empty, someone showed up with meat. When I had no groceries (even in that big house in that affluent neighborhood) and was in need, they brought armloads of groceries.

The scripture tells us in **verse 4, "your clothes did not wear out on you."** When my one-year-old was out of diapers, someone brought diapers. Others brought clothes and gave us money. When I was washing clothes with Palmolive (did you know you could do that?), someone brought laundry soap.

Verse 4 says **"nor did your foot swell on you these 40 years."** "Lord, don't let it last 40 years!!" Israel's mode of transportation was their feet; our mode of transportation was the Lincoln Towncar and the Aerostar

van. Just after my husband left his job, the company filed
bankruptcy. In his job, Brent had sold service agreements on
new electronics and appliances. Now hundreds of people
were holding worthless five- and ten-year service
agreements, for which they had already paid. A trustee was
appointed by bankruptcy court to liquidate any assets bought
with company funds. This included the equity in our home,
cars, and other properties. Everything was gone! We had
failed to follow the scriptural principle of storing up in the
years of plenty. We had no savings and were totally
unprepared. The company cars were gone. One person
purchased a car for us, complete with insurance and tag.
Another person provided a second car--a 1978 Camaro.

In 1978, I was in my first year of college, and didn't
have a car. I prayed, "Lord give me a car." I saw that God
gave other Christians things they asked for and thought He
wanted to do the same for me. I continued to pray, but there
was no car. Until now! A 1978 Camaro! Camaros are little
sports cars. Remember, I had driven a van and enjoyed

having my kids in the back of it, well out of my hearing distance.

I especially appreciated that car when one day I spotted a Mercedes being pulled by a wrecker. That little Camaro, by God's Grace, never failed to start or take us where we wanted to go. It was ugly, but God used that car to make me examine my sense of self-worth. I was unhappy with what I discovered. I was embarrassed to drive to church in that ugly car or be seen anywhere in it. God proved that He is faithful--and has a terrific sense of humor!

That Christmas we were the "needy family" in our church. We had given and now it was our turn to receive. That was hard, but I'm so glad God has taught us how to receive. One of my sweetest friends said, "If God calls us all to give, somebody's going to have to be on the receiving end of it sometimes." God had us, as Ron Dunn says in his book "Don't Just Stand There, Pray Something," in the school of hard knocks. We had to learn to receive. It is most embarrassing to be in need. The most uncomfortable gift that Christmas came from my uncle. We were not particularly close since he is an Army colonel and he and his family have always lived in another state or country. The gift was a check for $1,000. After they left, Brent and I wept over their generosity and over our own selfishness. I never would have given away that much money, especially at Christmas, since we had so many gifts of our own to buy!

Job 2:10 says, **"Shall we indeed accept only good from God and not adversity."** In **Chapter 42, verse 5,** Job says, **"I have heard of Thee, by the hearing of the ear, but now my eyes see Thee."** Job knew what God was like; now He could see Him.

That's what I want to convey to you. I have told you about the hard stuff, but what I most want you to remember is that God is sufficient. Through the trials, I have seen Him and have come to know Him better than I've known Him in my life. As crazy as it might seem, Brent and I thank God for the trials. If we had to do it again, we would be willing to walk through these troubled months with the Lord carrying us and our church family helping us.

Brent tried several jobs and although our situation improved somewhat, he was unhappy. He was unemployed when the church announced an upcoming mission trip to Brazil. You will recall that Brent had felt led to the mission field many years ago. He wanted to go on this trip, but we simply couldn't afford it. A member of our church felt led to pay Brent's way to Brazil. It was an answer to prayer.

While he was away, my prayer was that God would give Brent direction for his life. Several days after he left, Brent called and told me that he had the opportunity to stay for a few extra weeks. I couldn't believe it. Didn't he realize what it was like here at home? He still had no job, and there was no money! Did he not want to come home? Had God heard my prayer?

During my prayer time one morning, God let me know He was in control. He **had** answered my prayers. He was calling Brent to the ministry. I knew He was also calling me. Early in our marriage, we had considered going into the mission field; and now God was opening the door for us.

Brent returned from Brazil and applied for admission to a Christian seminary in New Orleans. In a few short months we moved to New Orleans to begin a new life.

Brent has a job now for which he is so well suited. God's Word explains it in **Ephesians 3:20: "to Him who is able to do exceeding, abundantly beyond all we ask or think."** He is a Pastor. It's possibly the most difficult job he has ever had, but he enjoys every moment of it. He is back in school, studying for his Master of Divinity degree.

Oh the joy of following Jesus! He uses our lives to illustrate the truth of His Word, to show us His sufficiency. The Bible tells us in **Acts 10, Galatians 2,** and **Romans 2** that God shows no partiality and is not a respecter of persons. You cannot say, "God did it for her, but He won't do it for me." Whatever he does for me, He does for you. He is sufficient for everyone!

And remember, the next time you are helping with Vacation Bible School and feeling like a glorified "baby-sitter," please realize there could be someone there like me

to whom you have the privilege of introducing Jesus Christ!
. . . it can make all of the difference in the world!

Lori Trice, the wife of a pastor in Berwick, LA, is the mother of three children. Lori and her husband Brent are working on their requirements to become appointed to the Foreign Mission Board. They hope to serve in Brazil.

Epilogue

Bonnie, Margolyn, Pat, and Lori hope that you have felt the Lord's presence as you have read their stories.

If you prayed to invite Jesus Christ into your heart while reading this book, they would like to hear from you and send you a booklet as you begin your new life in Christ.

Write to:

Milton Publishing Co.
P.O. Box 6
Lookout Mtn., TN 37350